The Truth of Houses

The Truth of Houses

Brick Books

Library and Archives Canada Cataloguing in Publication

Scowcroft, Ann, 1961-
    The truth of houses / Ann Scowcroft.

Poems.
ISBN 978-1-926829-67-8

I. Title.

PS8637.C698T78 2010   C811'.6   C2010-907673-7

We acknowledge the Canada Council for the Arts, the Government
of Canada through the Canada Book Fund, and the Ontario Arts
Council for their support of our publishing program.

The cover image is by Geoffrey Bawa, courtesy of David Robson and
the Geoffrey Bawa Trust.

The author photograph was taken by Maria Tsolka.

The book is set in Minion and Museo Sans.

Design and layout by Alan Siu.

Printed and bound by Sunville Printco Inc.

Brick Books
431 Boler Road, Box 20081
London, Ontario N6K 4G6

www.brickbooks.ca

For my sons,
and for Jonathon

Contents

Wanted   13

Thirty-nine   15

Dear Leah   17

Kathy   20

Late chinook   22

Poise   24

À la belle soeur   25

Phantom   27

Learning   28

One morning near Boston   30

Stillness   32

Foreigner   33

Letter to my mother   37
(Palimpsest)

   i.   true or false: it is dangerous for a mother
        to expose the root of a lie   41

   ii.   your memory   43

   iii. your brain   44

   iv. the wind   45

   v.   there's a funny story my mother
        used to tell   46

   vi. summer of 1942   48

   vii. some things other things about the brain   49

   viii. clue   50

ix.   whether it is appropriate to claim that an event
      is only meaningful in context   51

x.   fifty/love   53

xi.   in which the power of revision is discovered   55

xii. across the highway and past the prison,
      north of Detroit we go   56

xiii. in which the potential downfalls of consumer
      desire are revealed   58

xiv. further qualities of the hippocampus   59

xv.   in which we discover life does not unfold like a novel,
      with resolution following climax   60

xvi. scrabble   62

The truth of houses   67

Call and response   68

Whether it is possible to travel without possessions   69

Atakkāvacara (beyond logic)   70

Āhāra (nutriment)   72

Observation   73

Acariya (closed fist)   74

Checklist   76

Selected excerpts from the atlas of desire   78

i.   definition   78

ii.   summer of rain   80

iii. six ways to sublimate the rain   81

iv.   corollary   83

v.   wind rising   84

Rough translation of Ronsard's *Mignonne*   86

Quotidian   91

April   92

Addendum to Dear Leah   94

Forty-two-year-old woman takes tennis lessons   95

Second storey   96

Immaculate wing   98

Love poem   100

Red Volkswagen   102

How to begin   104

Dukkha (suffering)   105

Residuum   107

Grandmother, sewing   108

Winter forecast   109

First birth   110

First child leaves home   111

What remains   112

Acknowledgments   115

Biographical Note   117

… this seeming chaos which is in us is a rich, rolling,
swelling, dying, lilting, singing, laughing, shouting,
crying, sleeping *order*. If we will only let this order guide
our acts of building, the buildings that we make …
will be the forests and meadows of the human heart.

Christopher Alexander,
The Timeless Way of Building

Wanted

Give me a hollowed cricket
summoning its mourning brethren inside these walls to sing.
Give me fist-sized spiders meandering like wayward cattle
across jungle roads.
Give me rosary beads across the back of knees,
sheep-tainted soil,
moons carved from wood on clouded nights,
your photos in the box, waiting.
Give me strawberry fool and crisp loaves
baked at dawn by a woman in another country.
Give me leaves sending their green back into the bevelled trunks of trees,
oily sturgeon,
your brother gone to a Christ you will never know.
Give me traffic jams from New York City to Springfield.
This name: *Gurumaan.*
The knowledge of how young we once were
and may be yet.
Pour it now, the world entire:
the frightened police,
the men intoxicated by mayhem,
the spike-haired boys who gently lifted your father
that day downtown.
How is it we can never remember
nothing is as it seems
or ever was how we truly remember it?
Your daughter's face in the cup of your palm,
the schools turned into prisons,
how beautiful my name sounds in your mouth.
Pour it in, pour it into the sieve of these jugged ears

and I will return it real as the ocean calling through
pine scrub at new moon,
the knife's first slice into pumpkin flesh,
the fact your breathing and dreams
go on despite you.

Thirty-nine

When I was six I planned to marry Jack Plucket,
of the dark hair and rosy cheeks. We would
have five children: two boys, three girls.
At thirteen I knew I would grow up
to teach eighth grade English and marry Paul Crawford,
who would teach Shop in a larger version of himself.

At sixteen my future turned to Butch Meyer,
a rangy pimple-faced swimmer with an overbite
I couldn't get enough of in the sharp grass
of Lake Michigan dunes, Saturday nights after enough
Strohs to make me bold, though
he wouldn't talk to me in the light of day.
At eighteen I imagined a new life
and thought that meant not kissing boys,
destiny being more complicated than I had imagined.

Clearly lacking cachet, at twenty I moved to Paris—
but Ernest and Zelda, Gertrude and James were gone
and the only boy who wanted to kiss me
drove a bus to spite his parents,
worked hard to smell of petrol and Stella Artois.

It would appear I never quite had a plan beyond
certain adoration, contentment and later, just maybe,
a cultivated smattering of fame.
Which is perhaps why I never imagined myself at thirty-nine,
fighting my disappearance into wife, mother, teacher—
common nouns with voracious appetites and poor digestion.

Je suis comblé.

It never occurred to me I would have to gestate my life again,
that the angst of adolescence could return, that I could
step up to the mirror on a cold September morning,
see clearly all that had come before,
yet nothing, nothing of what lies ahead,
the putty of which sits shapeless yet
in the palm of my hand.

Dear Leah

I have not answered your letter,
penned in block letters, then
torn from a spiral notebook.
The return address says Huron Street, but
the first sentence reads
I've been institutionalized again,
a greeting that lies as quiet and plain
on the page as my own
standard weather report.
The meat is an account of the whereabouts,
occupations and progeny of siblings,
none of which has changed dramatically
since we became roommates, twenty-one years ago
in the last all-girl dormitory on campus.
Write if you like, you offer as a close,
tell me what your family are up to.

❖

You were working at the Tool and Die
in our hometown,
not living a fresh life with a fine lover
in Wisconsin as I'd imagined
in my twelve years of maladjusted domesticity,
and since our last reunion.
170 pounds on your five-foot frame,
stubble on your chin from the last time
you shaved, days ago.
Your right leg banged involuntarily
on the underside of the kitchen table
as you ate the burger you'd carried clutched
in your damp fist up the mirrored elevator
to my mother's apartment.

Later, when we walk the pier alone,
you plug your lower lip with chaw,
spit its juice carefully into a paper cup.
You walk as if we were on ocean bottom,
each step deliberate
and exhausting.

The summary of despair takes five short minutes:
betrayal again
then again.
The first institution voluntarily,
the next at the end of a rope
pulled by your six brothers.
Poverty, debt—
lithium, lithium, lithium.

Without advice to dispense,
I am in foreign territory.
I have spent the last nine years failing
to resolve squabbles two short boys have
over the territory of Lego.
What comes next in this conversation?
You shuffle along, neither content nor dissatisfied.
I endure the silence as I would a short illness,
long for the sticky touch of my children's
fingers around my neck,
the compact heat of their bodies next to mine.
I want you to leave for the job
you will lose within two weeks.

Leah,

Last week my sons arrived
at my desk in the euphoria of discovery.
They'd been careful to choose
who got to tell the secret
beforehand, so as not to ruin
the moment.
The youngest, who had navigated
half a mile
with the perfect blue egg
cradled in the cup of his palms
produced it now with such flourish
it escaped his protection.
He nearly caught it twice,
and then it lay broken,
miniature white and yolk
just an ordinary mess now.

His grief was immediate and profound.
I rocked him in my arms
but all I could find to say was
I know, I know.

Kathy

That summer, you and I hobbled up the gravel road,
our hips and shoulders twisting as though jagged swaggering
would reduce the impact of stones
on the still-soft soles of our feet.

We wore new bathing suits. For me,
a thick polyester one-piece; for you,
a halter bikini that barely contained your genuine breasts,
buoyed already in air.
We rolled semi-truck inner tubes past the cornfield on the right,
bungalows on the left, trees along the river's edge screening
all but glimpses of its cool promise.

We could take the short route down to the boat launch,
throw our tubes in there for half a lazy ride, or
we could brave the field and bush, take the whippet lash
of thistle and begin across from the island—as a reward,
surreptitiously witness the backyard lives of our neighbours,
listen to Mr. Falwalk yell at his wife,
theorize why Mrs. Taylor never left her two-storey palace,
scorn the one-upmanship of Long's floating dock
over your wooden pier.

And between yards there were always boys
and what you did to them and what they did to you
when you let them and the fabulously complicated politics
of the when you let them. So,
one chapter in my apprenticeship
to womanhood, this careful, uninformed regard,
this list compiled for the pleasure of ticking off
as we planned our prospects, embraced by the slightly diesel hold
of those inner tubes, twirling down the lazy river,

our mouths full of knowing unadulterated by experience,
your body ripe, mine yearning,
the future just around the next bend
predictable and sure.

Late chinook

It is late April, later than snow
should lie calf-deep in woods I call
ours, as I think of those boys as ours,
the ones who run ahead on this first possible
walk of spring, this first unencumbered meander
through forest and across a wan, bent mat of hay,
far too involved with absorbing thaw's slow shock
to send any envoy of fresh shoots just now;
even the valiant ferns unfurling in concentric
circles at the wetland's edge still wear their
dun capes, as if travelling disguised into
this unsure season.

The boys rediscover each camp, each fort,
each hideout, each long day of last year's
summer; they repair and plan for the future
while I scout for evidence
of all I have missed in the long months our land
keeps its secret life from us, as a mother will hold
her other life quiet in the centre of her body until
her children are asleep.

First there is the usual: opened mouths
of mouse homes in soggy, collapsed hay,
curlicues of rust-coloured porcupine scat
at the base of a white pine; sapling branches
stripped beyond their green by hungry deer;
cottony pods of larvae pressed deep between
new and old skins of a beech in its last season;
owl pellets of mole fur and shrew bone.

The archaeology of true drama begins on the southeastern slope.
Clumps of rabbit fur lie immune to a rising wind,
pulled from dermis as you might pull fibres from an artichoke
to reveal the pocked, dense meat of the heart.
A severed fox claw perfectly preserved.
The hollowed skull of a grinning weasel.

Up along the eastern fence line I notice a fluid
ripple of white, an incongruous flutter,
as if the land was remembering November and the release
of milkweed parachutes. On approach,
perfect individual underfeathers come into focus,
cling in a rippling breeze to barren stalks of dogwood,
and I remember my son running to greet me
one afternoon in the dead heart of February,
his face shining with the story of how
there was one swift shadow just outside the kitchen window,
and then another—by the time he and his father
could stand to see, the young eagle had a snow goose
clutched in its talons. My son saw the moment its beak nestled
into the goose's neck, saw droplets of blood falling;
when finally they were dressed and out the scuffle
was over—they arrived just in time to see the eagle heave
its shoulders and take the air. *We didn't find one bone,*
he said, *not one bone.*

Standing now at the eastern fence line
the down fluttering in a late chinook,
I think of that boy's father and the years we've shared,
and I marvel at the heart's stalwart nature,
its foolish hope
that we have come to spring for good,
and at last.

Poise

My son, draped in a towel outside the tub,
weeps and blood
streams from the rent in his knee,
from the small open mouth of wound on his knee and
the water and blood flowing together make it appear
worse than it is. He stands there, his leg
a series of bloody tributaries, a large stain blooming
on the bath mat, his lips stretched tight against
the prospect of sutures—
such a moist word you can already hear the sound

of the needle as it punctures his skin. You can almost
see the clinically-tired emergency room doctor
who has worked all day and will work all night,
who will be coughed on and complained to, you can
almost see her before my boy,
just another boy on another Sunday night with another
knee split open, he can't exactly remember how
although surely, probably, it was his brother's fault.
You can almost hear that doctor sigh

as you look at my ten-year-old boy, his knees
bolting the slender bones of his legs together,
his body in seeming poise despite the
microscopic gears and pulleys at work
in blood in sinew instructing his body how
to grow away from me just as he nears
my height. When will it stop, this
abject, necessary collapse against my chest,
how many more times will he accept this intimate comfort
before his body closes around itself in its perfection,
before he takes his position in my blind spot
like a dream I knew I had and once,
almost remembered.

À la belle soeur

Montréal cul-de sac, townhouses
like so many private-school boys in a row.
A night for clogs full of rain
and the discovery once inside
that except for their soggy heels
my socks don't match.

We enter the home of the artist's sister,
are offered dry white wine.
Breakfast nook, reading nook.
Books and indigenous sculpture tastefully placed
on spotless glass tables.

The artist's wood blocks and paintings
deserve their awards.
Like the poems I most admire,
they are spare and quiet.

During the artist's discourse
on creative process,
on painstaking detail,
on failed attempts with exorbitant materials,
my eyes, while pleased by the watery,
perfectly disturbed image
of a sparrow's river reflection,
are drawn increasingly to corners,
lampshades, to the under under of couches,
where there is no dust.

I find myself searching for *la belle soeur*
because we haven't been introduced,
because I want to sweep my hand and proclaim:

You have children who deliver hors d'oeuvres
in clean white shirts
and ties without clips,
and while they are not gracious
not one chewed as he served.

And you, while certainly you hired help
to vacuum up soldiers under the table
and wash the wall behind the stove
and hide the clutter of family in too-few closets,

it was you who hollered about toothpaste
dried to caulk in the bathroom sink,
hounded days on end
to present this immaculate gesture,
which I would like you to know

did not go unnoticed.

Phantom

This is good-bye.
This is your first step forward.
This is your blood rattling with the new.

A child conceived in dreams of fear and longing
yet never born
leaves a trembling gap between two stars.

This void won't be satisfied with leftover rice,
loosened buttons, dog bones, undone screws, empty milk cartons—
not even with bark unfurled from the paper birch.

It doesn't desire animal, mineral, vegetable.
It has one hunger—the translation of
O—

Thinness of your father's legs before you admit
he is dying,
wobbly stalk of your month-old child.

And this from now
until you pull that gap tight behind you
upon your own departure.

Learning

Kate and Tom go to the beach.

Kate and Tom like the beach.

Here are Kate and Tom.

Surely you can see me,
lower lip dropping deliberately to find the
K in Kate, exposing my incisors past the *a*
(which says its name), then clamping firmly
on *t*.
This is hand-cranked language
issuing mutely from my mouth,
poised above the heat of my son's head,
which nestles in the crook of my arm and is followed
directly by his delicate neck and slender body,
which doesn't want to be here
decoding for my benefit.

I mouth at his excruciating pace
trying, in the space between words,
to remember when English might have been Cyrillic,
the whim of *ea* making *e*,
the nonsense of *w* in *w*rite,
and remember feeding him at seven months,
my own mouth opening as he accepted the spoon,
closing as he received it.

Why did I not crawl before him when he could only rock,
frustrated and inconsolable on the parched kitchen floor?
Why did I not walk with exaggerated deliberation—
heel sole ball toe lift, repeat—
when he clung to the furthest edge of anything

desperate to go forward alone?
And when will I be so compelled again
to mimic what he holds already in his body, waiting?

Surely you can see me,
there in the bushes
outside his girl's house, the only girl
in a world full of girls.
His arm drapes around her shoulder,
her head rests in the crook of his arm,
and I am not speaking these words:
Love me.

One morning near Boston

A man walking home too quickly from Synagogue,
one daughter quiet, the other yowling and
hanging just back, so he must pull her, his head bent
forward in that determined way a man careful about the fall
of his coat can have. I try to meet the girls' eyes in a way that
won't deepen their shame or drive shame's wedge deeper
into their father, who is so much larger and will
shut the door when finally they reach home.

In my coat pocket I carry arnica, which I dispense, among
other places, at hockey games to boys whom other boys
have smashed into the boards, sent wobbling back
to the bench. The fathers rattle change in their pockets
and look away as I tap three small white grains into mouths
still taught to grin and bear. I wish I had a remedy for the
father pulling his daughter behind, a gesture that could
spring from my hand and relieve his shame so
he might stop his determined walking, drop his head back
and wail at the exhaustion of little girls, their tiny politics
and miniature treacheries, their bottomlessness when
he has learned so carefully to live with meagre; and

in this world where a gesture to relieve shame
springs from my hand, doors open up and down
Commonwealth Avenue and, like canines drawn to the moon,
parents and grandparents, spinster aunts, incontinent
great uncles who also just lost their drivers' licenses, two-
timing husbands, girls with ugly red infections in places their
mothers warned them not to puncture, mailmen who thought
that way they could also be novelists, forty-year-olds everywhere,
their mortality newly risen on the horizon, single mothers startled
awake again by the diurnal blossoming anxiety in their chests,
the overextended, the underemployed, the pizza boy hopelessly in love,

the dispossessed, the disengaged, the disheartened, the disturbed,
the dissociated, everyone,
everyone begins to keen good and long until finally
there are only snivels until finally

the man can look down and see his daughters,
see the face of his beloved wife in their faces, the eyes
of his mother in their eyes, until
he notices the delicious warmth of the wind—
and in March of all months!

Until he notices
the pronged red buds
on the delicate fingers of the maples,
until something somewhere
replaces the earth on its axis
then spins it gently
so that it might rejoin the stately waltz,
revolve in what must be exquisite silence
without us.

Stillness

Some mornings I wake already
bored by a head full of banter that has chased me
across sleep into dream, so that chattering still
upon waking, it seems I haven't slept, so
yesterday hasn't finished and today, look— I'm
already behind even as I lean
to gather my son into my arms, feel
the sweet warmth of his sleep rise
against my neck, *forgot to write the*
cheque rings in the left forward quadrant
of my brain, the synapses of forgetting
being the first to wake, you didn't call,
didn't write, didn't wash, didn't find,
didn't remember remember remember

when the midwife handed that boy over?
Sticky, wet, he seemed surprised to find
himself here. His passage had been sudden
and difficult. I'd lost touch with him
several times travelling the folds of my own pain.
It is nearly impossible to hold the image
of his journey, his skull collapsing, the total
giving over his body had to endure, and then
the air here, the long wide world,
and all that must be learned over and over again—
especially forgiveness.
Especially the flowering of the heart.
Especially the still moment,
which is all some of us will ever understand
as God.

Foreigner

Turn on the light, her husband entreats,
sensing her form, upright again,
ready for launch into solitude
or, he fears, despair—
not understanding the comfort
of navigating by memory, taste, smell,
the texture of the third worn stair.
Clear vision, she once told him,
is overrated. It was like telling a bird
there is also oxygen in water.

Her childhood, for example,
cannot accurately be explored from squares
of smiling birthday or class pictures.
Better stone-studded concrete
Saturday evening,
high August 1973 on a dead end road
near a muddy, swaying river.
The humidity glistens,
weighing even on mosquitoes that bobble distractedly
without a single breath of wind to propel them forward.
Water molecules so dense and whole in the air
that even the grass, by the law of like and like,
must leach its green up and diffuse,
wash the atmosphere in pale yolk.

Bullfrogs thrum in the marsh,
corn trembles growing in stillness.

From this Saturday perch she hears
her parents snoring.
She knows they lay sprawled,
having fallen again

from the precipice of their habit,
white sheets and blanket
bunched at their mute feet.

Here restlessness was born.
Fuel for a life apart.

... even when we have seen deep into the processes
by which it is possible to make a building or a town alive,
in the end, it turns out that this knowledge only brings us
back to that part of ourselves which is forgotten.

Christopher Alexander,
The Timeless Way of Building

Letter to my mother

We have years of words, decades
of clauses caught in the soft spots of our throats
where the skin is supple and concave;
they have massed in our vocal chords
disorderly, unruly—
sheer numbers make it difficult to breathe.

The sound you hear is not a rasp,
not the result of cold or strep.
It is an echo, listen:
the words are saying themselves in my throat.

And you? I always assumed it was emphysema,
but perhaps it is the breath constricted by your
own words, air whistling through
the crowded space of your best intentions,
of what you would
have said, of what you meant
to say, if only

(Palimpsest)

i.   true or false: it is dangerous for a mother to expose the root
     of a lie

Do you remember that day when bent
before me on one knee you snapped
shut the unforgiving plastic of my rain jacket
and with bemused indulgence recited:
Oh what a tangled web we weave,
When first we practice to...
deceive.
You had caught me lying, some inconsequential lie, perhaps:
Yes I ate the crusts.
No I never used your scissors.
The dog got mud on my boots.

I am five and anxious to be released into the wet
green yard with my new umbrella, which is transparent and
creaks when opened, smells of all that is new and mine
exclusively, through which I will watch the rain fall,
listen to the splot! plock! of each drop,
giddy in my bubble of vinyl vapour,
boots squelching, shins splattered.
Earthworms will rise in watery elevators
and I will extract one slowly, watch its accordion segments
strain, wonder will it snap free from earth's grip like
a rubber band on a sling, coil whole in the palm
of my hand or just snap then grow
another head or tail?
And will that happen right away?
Will I see?

But I'm lying again.
Did you notice the shift from past to present?
The slide from present to future?
Did you see the earthworm stretch?

That never happened,
yet I see it more clearly than most of my childhood.
If truth resides in details,
which details?

ii.   your memory

the man I know has left
and this other one pulls me on his knee
even his voice has changed
urgent, low
just come here a minute
he is consumed by something I cannot fathom
presses his trembling lips to mine
then holds me still
with one hand as the other explores my
narrow chest then pulls the elastic on
my underpants when
I strain for release he whispers in my ear *stay here*
I can tell he needs this but I am not stupid
I leave and watch what remains from the safety
of the meticulous
pressed tin ceiling

iii. your brain

For example, your fingers are the source:
reach for the damp forehead of your sleeping
child then lift to bring his smell into you;
your thalamus is the road, carrying this
information to the amygdala, which rates it
from one to ten then passes the moment to
your hippocampus, the secretary, which files
it next to the memory of that same child, soft
and aware at six months,
loving you with a completeness
you never even thought to imagine,
resting the impossible weight of his head on
your shoulder, caressing your face with one small
hand as you bend to bring all of him back
into you for the space of one breath one
inhalation of the sweet spot at the base of his
tender neck—

this sensation, this secret, this miracle,
Broca's area will translate,
bring to your mouth as clay.
From there, it is up to you.

iv. the wind

I stand next to him. He wears patched
coveralls and a straw hat.
He is pointing at the walnut's leaves, showing their grey-green
undersides, rattling in the south-easterly wind.
It's going to rain, he says, *you can tell by the leaves.*
I am six.
I believe him.
Everything he says is true.

v.   there's a funny story my mother used to tell

So—
she's been waiting and waiting and finally,
finally she gets the call. She's eight
months pregnant and isn't supposed to fly
but living with her parents these last months
she says, well, if only she'd have thought to eat
more beans she probably could have powered
over there all by herself she was so ready
to get the hell out.

When she gets to the air base
they tell her the plane isn't going to make it,
she'll have to wait until next week. One
look at her mother's trembling chin and she
points to a loaded transport and says: *Where's that
one going? This is an emergency.*

In Munich a skinny lieutenant named Eddy
drives her to the Bahnhoff and gets her on
the right train. She hasn't slept in thirty-six hours,
hasn't bathed in seventy-two. She is wrinkled and
tired, hot and smudged sore and
totally unsure if her young husband is
going to meet her in Nuremberg or how
she is going to know when to get off but
most of all, right now, she has to pee.

She lurches back and forth back and forth
led down the narrow corridor by the arrow
of her belly and the increasingly urgent demands
of her bladder, which she placates with constant

updates of estimated arrival, disengagement and
release schedules. Near the toilet a dapper porter
takes her by the elbow and asks
(here my mother uses her Colonel Klink voice):
Vant to haf a trink vis me later?
Unable to calculate this into the promises she
has been making to her body, let alone to bear even one
solitary image of sloshing liquid, immediately and consummately
enraged at this unsuspecting man, she blurts out the only
German word she knows: *Schnauzer*!

vi. summer of 1942

My mother is in hog heaven.
Her mother couldn't do a thing with her so sent her
here to be done something with. She won't
have to pick a single cherry all summer, or a
peach or a blueberry, no burnt neck and
sore back, no sticky steaming vats of
anything, no fifty-pound bags of sugar. No
Rocky either of course, but the first thing
her uncle did was give her a BB gun and tell her to belly
down in front of the barn and shoot rats. He
crouched next to her in his coveralls and
straw hat, pointed to the places vermin
could squeeze between the slats. *Nice*
to have a kid like you around, he said.
I know you're not afraid
of hard work.

vii. some things other things about the brain

If the amygdala is overwhelmed by an experience
the hippocampus doesn't know how to file it.
Like any six-year-old can tell you in these situations,
you should just stuff it under the bed
or behind the
door. No one will ever know unless
perhaps one
day your lover whispers in your ear,
just come here a minute.

viii. clue

the porter
in between the cars
with the pregnant woman

ix. whether it is appropriate to claim that an event is only meaningful
in context

And what of the comic possibilities?
Imagine those scenes if you could just
turn off the sound, speed up the chase
sequence: there's the lecherous old coot, his bald
pate reflecting back your sympathy for all that
comes undone in our lives, his body bent
to the child's height, his arms
cocked to his sides, loaded for the grab.

Cut to the Congregational church thrift
shop and the child's great-aunt folding other women's
discarded nylon petticoats. A scroll of text
tells us her mouth is saying,

"I thought she'd have more fun
with her uncle in the barns
than here all morning!"

Back at the farm, the child has made
it out the sprung screen door, down
dissolving concrete steps to the lawn.
The man watches her through the thin screen,
its holes mended in bright embroidery thread
to resemble the idea of flowers.

She watches him without watching
through her peripheral vision—
enough of the child left in her
at this moment to believe
what she cannot see does not exist.

With proper editing, you would feel
the triumph of her escape.
You could cut out entirely
the hours and hours
before her great-aunt returns.

x. fifty/love

Older now, you drop the names
of your lovers like crumbs
for your starving mother.

It will be years before you understand
the astonishment she feels
at your having grown into a life
without her.

Meanwhile, you watch, as if from a distance,
as the flare of your revelation
exposes a power you did not know you contained
and which you can wield like an iron bar
and do.

At that moment, when she is fifty,
and you find yourself revealing details
you have never told anyone,
she looks older than you'll ever remember her.

Is that when she tells you?
Is that when she rolls back that story you love
to the point where she lurches back and forth
back and forth led down the narrow corridor
by the arrow of her belly?

You on one side of the picnic table
watching the river swirl and eddy
so slowly you almost expect
it will pause to breathe,
your mother on the other side, cigarette
between two fingers of one hand

styrofoam-blanketed Schlitz
in the other,
her bridge player's mind having begun
the tack of this attack
at some distant moment back in the conversation,
perhaps the moment you realized you could let her watch
as you pulled loose, one by one,
the strings of her knowing you.

xi. in which the power of revision is discovered

Back and forth back and forth. It is chill
between the cars in September in Germany
in 1955. Nothing is quite yet repaired.
A stone house intact on approach
opens like a broken mouth
upon the train's retreat.
The head stinks
but she must go, and urgently.

The porter watches her approach
from his spring seat near the door.
How many broken mouths·
lie hidden behind his gaze in that country
saturated with stories beyond telling
we will never know,
but when he rises to push-slide the door
he does not then return to his half-sleep
on the spring seat
but makes a home for his hands
from my mother's body, her young woman's body,
eight months of child inside.

I am aced in that moment, near
the muddy river.
It will be twenty more years before
I put myself again into a position
where she can reveal her hand,
her strand of the tangled web,
its tensile strength as yet unmatched
by science.

xii.   across the highway and past the prison, north of Detroit we go

I am young enough to believe that at eighty, my great-aunt
is exceedingly old, so one visit determine it essential
to collect her on paper.

Her husband is long gone. I am young enough
to believe that dead, he no longer poses any threat.

Her eight brothers, my grandfather among them,
fill most of the pages, what with their wives
and children, their ailments and careers, the sunny
states to which they retired, the diseases
that crept into their bones and hearts while she,
                              stolid and barren
outlived them all.

Around her solitary sister I have drawn a box.
She never married, but aspired to perform
and taught piano when she wasn't
institutionalized.

She lived with us once, my great-aunt tells me—
after an episode is what I've underlined
in my college-ruled notebook. I am young enough
to believe this kind of thing only happened to
independent-minded unmarried women
in the pre-feminist millennia.

She lived with us once.
But she refused to stay.

My great-aunt sits at that hard-won farm-wife
extravagance: The Dining Room Table, with its
elegant bowed legs, its matching buffet. She bought

it with green stamps and jars of quarters.
I can easily imagine the catalogue picture in which
it appeared: a chandelier surely hung above it there,
its sleeved candlesticks bulbed with shapes of flame.
Here, flies buzz helplessly, stuck on curled
yellow glue papers suspended by cellophane tape from
the pressed tin ceiling.

She drums her fingers, then locks
my eyes, tells me her sister had said
while packing her bag,
Your husband is a prevert.

This is as close as we will go, this landscape of the
near-word; my aunt tells me without once opening
her mouth *there are certain chasms*
across which no bridge must ever be built and I am
young enough then to believe
this is true.

xiii. in which the potential downfalls of consumer desire are revealed

When my mother sent me to the farm my great-aunt
no longer had eggs to candle, stock to feed, stalls
to clean; nor yet any children or grandchildren to spoil, so
we drove in her spacious blue Oldsmobile to the Macomb Mall,
that lonely new Mecca squatting in some man's cornfield
about seven miles as the crow flies
but so far
from 1971 in Detroit.

And we were truly dazzled by the accumulated wares on display
and our separate desires were strong: for her, dishes
and more dishes thirty years too late to feed ten men three
meals a day; for me, the flimsy allure of undergarments
my mother had already snapped her purse shut against
in materials that slid across my palm
like the drop of mercury my sister kept
in a pill bottle on her desk.

I modeled for her, in stores that were not Sears, my
child's body transformed beneath the contraband garments.
Together, we selected a shimmering, clinging, one-piece
camisole that held itself tight by
hooks and eyes at the crotch.
Later, back at the farm she came
to my room and said, *Show him, won't you?*
I resisted, but not so long that she might guess why
and loathe me.

Had said while packing her bag *your husband is a
prevert.*

                                        Locked my eyes.

There are certain chasms.

This is as close.

xiv. further qualities of the hippocampus

It files all the memories
nevertheless,
somewhere safe,
lets them slip out
now and again in case
you are ready
to place them
where they belong,
in case you have
finally peeled away
their razor-sharp edges
with your tongue
by the telling.

xv. in which we discover life does not unfold like a novel, with
    resolution following climax

My mother sits in a white PVC tube chair
with an aqua cushion.
The wall behind her is white.
Heavy salt air has begun to erode
the fish sculpture on the white wall.
The corrosion is aqua.
So, I say, that most ubiquitous transition from one
unrelated subject to another,
there's this thing I want to tell you.

Alternately, I might have shouted, "Fire!"
or "Man overboard!" My mother pulled her legs
from their elevated repose, lit a cigarette,
jiggled the ice in her tumbler. Alternately she might
have shouted "Stop, thief!" or
"Because I said so, that's why!"

X abused me as a child, I state bluntly. What I
meant her to interpret was: "You know that man you
revered, the one for whom you named your only son?
Imagine the worst, and how at six,
I already knew I must not tell you."

Alternately, I could have said, "I have learned that in a situation
about which one must not speak, one can also
learn to be sly." The response I expected was
"I am sorry," except more so.

What she said instead was, *He did that to me too.*
The moment during which all oxygen
departed the planet only seemed long. *I've
never told anyone that*, she added.

Alternately, I could have said: "Language, like
muscle, can atrophy. By speaking around our
lives all these years, what we have left are pronouns,
helping verbs, some serviceable nouns and
a handful of adjectives. Therefore I say: 'How are you'
when what I have been waiting for you to hear is
'Please, help me.'" Therefore, while it would be logical
to pose the question: "Why?" followed perhaps by
"Why didn't you warn me?" or "Why did you let me go there
unprepared?"

I don't.

Beer? you ask, standing.

Yes, I say.

xvi. scrabble

This much I know is true:
my mother goes out, and before her
on the round white table are runs
and pairs and threes of a kind. *Rummy*,
she says, and before I can whimper she
looks me in the eye and says, *If I let you win
you'll never learn how.*

Thirty-five years later, at another round
white table, she places her tiles on the
scrabble board. Her focus is what I wish for
in meditation: only the word, this word,
and beyond that, in the background,
the game. Perhaps what she intended
to teach me all those years ago was fight.
What I learned instead was: let them win,
if it's so important to them.

In my dreams, there is danger
near at hand; perhaps a man with an axe,
perhaps a car with no driver. I struggle to
speak, can feel the words behind my teeth, the
pressure building in my chest and throat and then
I wake, descend the stairs of our sleeping home
to a kitchen flooded with January's full moon.
Outside, the paper birch casts its shadow across
blue snow. I slip on boots, a jacket, then step out
into the frigid air, wait for a sharp report to shoot
out from the frozen poplars, reverberate across the barn's
tin roof. There's something cleansing about a cold
this profound, and I breathe deeply.

When I first became a mother I could
not tell my son what he most needed to hear
upon waking from that other world of his
dreams. *I will always protect you. You are safe here,
with me.* How could I make such a promise? How?

I have since learned there is only one way:
to open my mouth,
and believe.

The quality which has no name includes these simpler
sweeter qualities. But is so ordinary as well, that it
somehow reminds us of the passing of our life.

It is a slightly bitter quality.

Christopher Alexander,
The Timeless Way of Building

The truth of houses

Tree houses

Tiered houses

Houses with towers and domes and cupolas

Shacks jerry-rigged on public land

The idea of houses
(self-contained)
where only the loudest dramas
are revealed to passers-by yet
which enfold absorb echo hold
still the memory of every emotion spent in voice or sweat
by its guarded inhabitants
skins rolled close over nerves as blinds roll
closed over square windows open windows
windows of rice paper and sapling branch
through which cold is kept out or heat in from which
the sun is banished or welcomed

All of which is to say: the houses aren't fooled
The houses know the five truths

The truth of light: you will see before you understand
The truth of motion: escape is an illusion
The truth of trees: your busy life will dissolve into the soil
The truth of windows: what protects can also maim

The truth of peace:
despite all the other truths
knowing will come to you wearing one hundred faces
contain you as once you contained your
own blood

Call and response

i. *the one hand*

Sometimes our room is bathed
    in the blue white of a falling moon
Sometimes it is only your soft breathing
    that fills it
It is never quite dawn, even the house
    sleeps
The night's wood will sometimes
    hold its shape in white ash until I open the stove door
I do not touch your goodness, held
    in the spaces between your sleeping breaths
In our blue white room
    in our room without moonlight
I hold my one hand in the other
    I hold my one hand in the other

ii. *imaginary life of the one hand*

Reaches for his stubbled face and
    draws his mouth to hers
slides down his belly and rests there
    waiting
takes him by the shoulder and shakes
    and shakes him
puts the car into 5th and drives to New Mexico
    by way of the Mississippi, for months
pulls on his fingers one after another
    until the children are released
grabs him by the collar while the mouth whispers
    do not lose me

Whether it is possible to travel without possessions

When I think *travel*, I think *shed*—
as in this skin into which I pour my life
by drop or downfall, away away
with the day-to-day,
the uninhabited rituals of morning,
the neediness of even a coffee cup,
with the hardened dust of fine grounds
just beneath its rim where milk foam lifted
but did not deliver them to your waiting mouth this morning.

In solitude I imagine all I might leave behind:
the oven's carbon husk, the iron smudge on
dishwasher walls, thickened work of spiders between
screens and glass of windows rarely used and more—
any moment you have pulled away from me,
my mother's sudden joy after all these years,
the memory of my father, his back to the vineyard,
a pheasant's joined feet in his grip,
its wings open as arms,
as though it had invited its death.
And our boys, their damp, compact heat,
how you have drawn me to you and then our sleep, apart,
each of us travelling labyrinths of separate dreams,

open as arms,
as though we didn't know where this would all lead us—
to *shed*.

Atakkāvacara (beyond logic)

Our home was small, square, secure
settled on the edge of a pond filled by cool
springs and surrounded by hayfields, a wetland
generous enough to accommodate a family of heron,
a tall pine grove, its floor soft with a hundred years of
needles. I knew that land's perimeter, its heart
more intimately than my own body. In summer friends would
lurch from the picnic table—their bellies full of grilled fish, wine,
asparagus, strawberry sorbet—to the edges of a massive
bonfire, *il y avait des bons mots et blagues en deux langues
et entre les langues il ne manquait rien,*
rien, and I could not contain the desire to leave, some
sturdy weed weaseling up through concrete, I began
to have an arsonist's dreams, the field aflame, the house
poised to combust.

Here the sidewalks heave and skew.
Heat descends at midday like some unexpected, impassive guest
arriving just in time for a meal you'd had no intention to prepare.
There is too much traffic belching too much black exhaust,
no one understands my stilted *patois,*
stray dogs lie as though dead in the roads by day
then bark all night, a bomb explodes
near my son's school, a man I admire is kidnapped, a beggar
is so grateful for twenty cents, my shame at this immeasurable,
there is no disguising the suffering around the perimeter,
at the heart, here it cannot be parsed

from jasmine releasing perfume after dusk,
the stillness of a forest monastery,
the total faith in gossip, in Ganesh,
in the road trip the river the gorge the rainforest,
the mountain on which the Buddha's step is remembered in gold.

Here there is no choice but to wash your eyes, to remember
you are not who you think you are, but less
but more, here I can embrace my foreignness
with the forgiveness of a stranger.

Āhāra (nutriment)

Obvious: anything cooked with lemon grass anything
sprinkled with fresh coriander anything for which
an essential ingredient is dew also raspberries or arugula
anything that sets your mouth on fire anything that cools
it anything you didn't cook yourself then young leaves from
dandelions broken through crusted snow how you crave
bitter after all that cold skinned stems of lotus flowers
sliced paper thin sprinkled with vinegar also bread from
ovens sunk in the earth groundnuts roasted in sand
flaming custards the lazy suspension
of cooled coconut water

Fundamental: a lover enfolding you as he sleeps the belly
ballast of a young child that child's abandoned collapse
in your arms how the body remembers from that moment on
when it bends to gather anything at all flowers firewood the
child himself grown beyond your height the territory
of one glass too many your wildness your
wildness the body inhabited by music the vocal chords resonating
in a small room full of women each singing only one note how
a friend can embrace you bring forth all you have held and
love you anyway how everything, finally, is reduced to arms and
your willingness to extend or be received by them

Difficult: silence
how you have dreamed the fathomless
eyes of your teacher how you have had to learn there has never
been a moment in which you were not forgiven how this means
you must learn to walk all over again without the counterbalance
of your misery every single day
how this means that sometimes now you can hear the
beauty of a crow feel tenderness for all that must collapse your
body your memory and above all
your delicately wrought plan to escape from here
unscathed

Observation

Just before the bomb exploded   (and

submachine gun fire separated some molecules of
air from the company of some other molecules
of air, making a path skyward through
layers of two-cylinder engine exhaust dust
heat fluorocarbons oxygen like your body makes a path
through water only swifter, more loud and also
containing the possibility of death and
the president's brother's mouth went dry
inside the limousine, separating him momentarily
from almost remembering what his wife had asked him
at breakfast and that other mother's son, dressed in a bomb,
understood the shy intimacy of doubt and belief
just before his head separated from his neck and landed,
largely intact, some distance from what remained
of his body, say a wrist or ankle
the remnants of a toe the street sweeper pushed forward
unaware later on with other oddments of rubble   some
molecules of air, parted on his approach, reunited
behind his orange vest just before the day moved on
into other days and our memories reassembled themselves
into stories we could account for: weight
velocity acceleration frictional force gravitational
pull has nothing on grievance, on grieving, either can
propel us forward either can propel us to lay down, lay down)

the koels *houp houped* and the crows mewled
in that strange way they have with their tongues
inside their horny beaks.

Acariya (closed fist)

Fingertips stained and sore
from hulling strawberries—
twenty kilos, an entire day in the
sandy field and every pot, bowl,
roasting pan in the house
mounded and fragrant in the gathering heat
between the rows, while occasionally
the carmine sheen of a fruit that would not
arrive home after this long day without
its small collapse into juice and mold
caused you to bring it to your mouth, hold its
overbright sweetness there. Unlike a child
your lips were not stained, the picking
of berries like swimming laps—sixty, eighty,
a hundred and twenty

      (finally you had to contain your hunger in that filthy pool
        a continental seizure away, finally admit this
          was no meditative act but rather forget, forget).

The beautiful, relentless sun, strings of muscle
between your shoulder blades tightening.
This and the flies. This,
and your hand stuttering at the sag of
a berry visited in the night by slugs or mice.

Now your fingertips dig stems, tug
until white hulls release with muffled sucks.
Juice runs a course from wrist to elbow.
A wobbling drip splashes intermittently
on the porch boards,
where the blade clattered hours ago.

Tree swallows begin to
sweep towards the pond as chickadees rise from
wild grasses edging the field. It feels your hand might
never be released from this gesture, twisting hull after hull
your hand hours in the shape
of a lightly closed fist.

       (which is all he can see when he walks up the steps—
        all he can see when he walks up the steps
        is the emptiness held there,
        away from him).

Checklist

After Navid Modiri

1. regarding biology

do your fingers deny what the mind had decided
and check themselves a hundred times within
the chamber of the hands not to not to
reach for the collar of his shirt the soft dissolve of
skin at the edge of his brow is there
no touch that is casual that does not send a riot
of signals through the endocrine
reducing you to chemistry
matter as conveyance of fluid and electricity
matter as desire?

    a.) always
    b.) sometimes
    c.) never

2. regarding speech

must the act of speaking become an act of gentle
avoidance a means of self-protection before
your own desire do you find yourself articulating
the circumference of a buried city but never the city itself all
that dust the shards out of which you have only just
willed your body to form, and for him, do you
choose words that paint the temple walls in falu
and ochre paint fish swimming from a crevasse far from the sea
so the buried city beautiful only in his imagination does

not rise its rubble its debris in the wind he inadvertently
unleashed by the gesture, only the gesture
of his hand?

    a.) always
    b.) sometimes
    c.) never

3. regarding gravity

is your goodness in question that
smug fortress
did you wake one morning to discover all
your most precious signifiers had adapted
to a new landscape grown feathers where a foot had been
teeth in places that had never been carnivorous
has *mustn't* become *please*
did the fundamental laws of physics shift
so that you could no longer be certain the earth
would rise, however subtly,
to meet you when you fall?

Did you fall anyway?

    a.) always
    b.) sometimes
    c.) never

Selected excerpts from *the atlas of desire*

i.   definition

This longing
is a blossoming first in the throat's hollow
then in the chest, nearly unbearable yet
imagine this day without—imagine a field of wheat
at noon, in August, without the fine motor capacity
of the pupil.

Leaning into it, sitting with it in stillness
there is loneliness,
a membrane beneath the skin through
which your ravenous blood drinks sun,
wind, a lover's finger tracing the bottom edge
of your lip
through which—

So perhaps this is an essential condition
like the heart's involuntary thump,
the pump pump of the lungs,
the ventricles pulsing—

And what has been done, shed,
what has been lost
to reveal it?

Leaning into into *into* the longing for someone
you cannot name or know by habit of seeing
makes for restlessness and walking, then walking

then finally running to discover there is only
the alphabet of the mouth: palatal, glottal, dental
bilabial, alveolar, velar, uvular the shapes in which
you can almost say—

❖

In the meantime, attend to bearing,
but not weight,
the beauty of things unravelling,
retort of tree limbs snapping under wet snow
or yellow poplar leaves dancing over that pheasant's
jewelled body in late October sun
at the edge of a freshly graded road,
how for a moment those leaves
were ripples of feather beneath which muscle gathered
so that you waited expectantly
for it to rise and fly again.

ii. summer of rain

Again woken by rain
she imagines herself a river
he might swim in,
imagines she has woken this way
every morning for months,
her life a monsoon,
the rain from fingers of cloud
sweeping across her
(mostly water already)
as though it were his hands.

There's another man, a farmer so desperate
to save his second planting of soft-hearted lettuce
from the mouths of deer, he went out to meet them
one dusk, stripped naked as they paused in their grazing,
dropped to his knees in the mud, and carefully explained
what was his, what was theirs.

As for our lady of the rain,
it is that moment of hope, the farmer walking back
to his house, muddied and vulnerable,
his heart cracked open to admit
both himself and the deer,
in which she most believes,
so she wishes on lost pennies, considers
feng shui, then casts the memory of a face, a mouth
away from her a hundred times a day.

She does not know how to step into the mud,
speak rather than believe in words
that might result
in his hands on the softness of her belly,
the water of kisses
the rain, and then again.

iii. six ways to sublimate the rain

1.
Describe the field in spring.
Its exhausted hay.
Its fallen vetch.
Frost heaving up stones bigger than your head.
Cakes of iced snow.
Owl pellets, weasel skulls.
All things that will be green
        clenched in fists.

2.
Describe the bitter of fresh dandelion leaf.
Tannin in those fiddleheads you forgot to soak.
The velvet sun of nasturtium on your tongue.
Disappointment when there was no revelation of violet
in the candied violets.
Green wood in an unripe pear.
Earth of onions, garlic, cumin.
How you know loam should taste
when it sits fragrant and humid in your cupped hands.

3.
Describe the velar murmur of the cat, mouth full of sparrow.
Rivulets of thaw purling beneath the soil.
The sharp crack of air hundreds of feet above J—
when a raven lost the current's edge and flapped once
in perfect Arctic silence.
The insect pitch of spring peepers.
The excruciating patter of rain against lake skin
from the perspective of a trout.

4.
Describe the weight of your child's sleeping head.
Its radiating heat.
How, eyes closed, you thought that silk
was water on your arm.
Soft-skinned boulders beneath your numbed feet
navigating the river too early in spring.
The feathery reach of tamarack against your cheek.
His hand, drawing your face to him.

5.
Describe the smell of iron a tomato releases
when snapped from its stem in late August.
The iron in melting snow.
In freshly turned earth.
On the birth bed of your children.

Or, the sweet flora behind their necks
before they drank in anything other than you.

6.
Admit there is no rain.
Just your desire, blunt like a stone
and blind.

One meaning of *to bear* is carry.
One meaning
is to yield.

iv. corollary

Everything
outside that secret was muffled. Everything
inside a constant rushing in the ears like
being camped permanently next to
spring rapids, so that often it was necessary
to tip her head and ask people to repeat
themselves.

The secret was given up by consensus among:

1) The body that grew weary of its own yearning
one morning then the next, suddenly years,
all that shame, those tears, that desire.

2) The mind that grew weary of observing it
morning after morning on the hard seat
so that shooting pains in the spine
became a welcome point of focus.

3) The heart that knows
it is only one of the mind's lenses
but hungers deep in the belly anyway.

Arguably it is a choice to fall in love. Therefore let
us hope the corollary is that one might choose to
fall back out, learn to live in the body as a collection of
knees, elbows, hips, shoulder blades, jumble of bones
knocking around inside the skin without protection
from the great wide world in all its beauty.

v.   wind rising

In the dream my body is a mandala,
everything laid down by chance
or miracle or intent—

that first cell dividing,
the milky white eye growing elliptically,
the sex a large blossom and later,
bones elongating in an elastic skin
then also tears and laughter, the first boy
who put his mouth to mine, pride, fear,
desire, my own children growing within me,
without me, every time I have placed my hand
on his chest and waited for the heart's leap,
all of it in the dream becomes sand—
burnished saffron, ochre, cadmium, umber,
and the wind is rising.

Waking I watch the dream leave, rub
my feet together, feel their rough contours. My
son will hold these feet in his hands, fascinated
and appalled, like things made of clay
beginning to crumble—except it is me, his
mother. How he traces the ropey veins in my hands
with his index finger, shoves them around a little,
and how tender when I close my thumb in a
drawer, fall on ice.

My own surprise is this discovery: as obvious charms
diminish, flatten, chip, the first bones
left exposed are those of my longing—
white, sharp, porous, more thirsty
now than even the soft flesh of my young self
reaching to bring that boy into me,

to resolve me. Once I would have wanted to know
you, be known, solved—
now I only want to be held at the bone,
unknow myself,
nearly find you to lose you at once.

Rough translation of Ronsard's *Mignonne*

Mignonne, allons voir si la rose
      Hey, old man
Qui ce matin avait déclose
      I have already disclosed
Sa robe de pourpre au soleil,
      my rose since a long time
A point perdu cette vêprée
      just not to you
Les plis de sa robe pourprée,
      carpe diem always reminds me
Et son teint au vôtre pareil.
      of fishing with my brother

Las! voyez comme en peu d'espace,
      but you know what I'm talking about
Mignonne, elle a dessus la place,
      I'm hovering just before
Las, las ses beautés laissé choir!
      that moment my edges
O vraiment marâtre Nature,
      turn rust, just a little
Puisqu'une telle fleur ne dure
      I can see blowsy on its way
Que du matin jusques au soir!
      petals thrown open like arms in surprise
Donc, si vous me croyez, mignonne,
      pappus and anthers blown off my domed receptacle
Tandis que votre âge fleuronne
      there's no point telling what my body endured
En sa plus verte nouveauté,

to ripen these breasts, sweeten this bellyflesh, musk my sweat
Cueillez, cueillez votre jeunesse:
in this moment of pause before the end of all that
Comme à cette fleur, la vieillesse
in this moment when, finally, I am beautiful and strong at once
Fera ternir votre beauté.
and so full of desire I will burst

Come touch me. Come see.

If I consider my life honestly, I see that it is
governed by a certain very small pattern of events
which I take part in over and over again.

Christopher Alexander,
The Timeless Way of Building

Quotidian

In this square old house with warped wooden floors
and prim wainscoting, we have sown
plenty that slips between the cracks,
like so much birdseed spilled on the way in the door.

Dinners on time.
Laundry gathered, washed, hung, folded, sorted, put away.
Beds made.
The this, the that.

Perhaps routine is only subterfuge,
a smoke mightily fanned to hide a fear
bigger than the far side of space and nestled purplish blue
between our lungs.

How easily its seed takes between floorboard cracks
in a dry wooden house that shakes in the wind
as if it yearns for release from its stable mooring,
as if it might choose to rise like a powerful wizard
and fly away towards unknown lands.

April

There is a farmer who roots his thickest despair
in April mud, who squats in his fields before dawn
not having slept the night for spring's torment
rising just beyond his reach in dreams.
The wet grey soil,
the drained grasses having to wake again.
Who will ever know if birth is a joy for the born?
Imagine that long journey for which it is best
to be small and elastic.
Imagine that journey.

❖

Imagine Aunt M. sitting on her bed that April morning, five a.m.
curtains ill-fitting against the seventh floor window.
She is disoriented.
She believes she must be sick but it is so
much more
that April morning in the room with the ill
fitting curtains.
This is the other journey about which you will also
have no memory.
Imagine,
between you and me and she,
she is the first.

❖

I live my life here pitched forward,
every April walk at an unnatural angle,
pretend I didn't clench my eyes shut
to disappear March,

rolling up days beneath my own feet.
I was not raised Christian and so joyful for return,
but among farmers who drew their deepest breaths
in April,
who paused to feel the pleasure of sun at the shed's southeast corner
and knew even within that moment
neither this birth nor any before it
was a gift less than struggle.

Addendum to Dear Leah

On the other end of the phone your voice is bright.
Soon you'll finish the nursing degree
you began thirty years ago.
Meds still keep you sleeping for hours,
slow your metabolism. The extra weight
tethers you to the earth.
There are certain kinds of love
unthinkable now
because of the wild falling in from yourself.

And somewhere soon
your intimate understanding of a life lived
within and without the excess density
of dopamine, serotonin, norepinephrine
will allow a parent
whose daughter has become lost
inside the chemistry of her own brain
to be held, at least for a moment,
in the comfort of your knowing.

And what I knew?
Fear, as usual.
My familiar.

Forty-two-year-old woman takes tennis lessons

The coaches step onto the court glistening, as if
fresh from molds for the perfect specimen.
Their bodies lead. Their bodies
are the most excellent students.

Follow through, no, follow through
No—follow through. Steve demonstrates over and over
as my mind holds the picture of his fluid movement,
the immaculate trajectory of the neon ball. Still
my racket stalls in a place I don't remember leading it.

And so it has begun,
le décollage, the ungluing, the take-off.
Right here I begin my fickle crawl,
my obsequious service
to the neglected temple.

Imagine my ignorant surprise that the body
succumbed to all those years of loathing and now
must be loved, dimpled and pocked, swollen and stretched,
limping several paces behind the mind's command.

The surprise of discovering
I must depend upon my body,
believe blindly that its turn to run my life
will result in forgiveness.

Second storey

What to do about the son who clings,
remembers when night falls how Achilles
in that movie leapt into the air,
found his challenger's throat and sliced it open.
Or that ogre two movies ago
that rose from the slime full born and inviolable
or the one—what about—with the man who had
sharpened blades of steel instead of teeth. He says
they are all outside his second-storey window
in the middle of our land, which rises and falls
like the breath of some sleepy, ruminating mammal.

Close your eyes, I tell him, imagine our home in daylight.
The ducks in the pond, the smell of hay in the sun.
Listen to how the forest sings back the peepers' chorus.
Sometimes, he whispers, I am even afraid to breathe.

And what makes us safe, and what makes a home,
and what lies beneath the monsters that would
consume him without my protection, despite the noise
of my pages turning, my water drunk volubly
from just across the hall?

A week ago I walked the floodplains of my childhood,
again swatting clouds of insects, sucking my feet out of silt,
meandering through gullies of cool air that held the same sudden
surprise as springs in a pond or lake, trusting my body to remember
its way through red pine, maidenhair, violet, buttercup, dogwood,
Indian pipe to the bank of the lazy river
where I had found refuge from the ache of home
by immersion in the muddy chatter of that place.

At dusk I discovered that failing light
transformed everything into scrub and muck,
the path into a thousand unknown paths.

I am grateful my body learned so well to intuit escape,
but for my son,
I wish it could recognize home and then,
the way there.

Immaculate wing

Her father wore his underwear
where it belonged,
elastic tight across a protruding belly
hard like a birth, or a tumour,
loose about his thinning legs,
from which she averted her eyes.
It was not the dying she minded so much.
It was being held witness to the slide.

(Even now she is deaf
to her hopeful son,
and the starling baby fallen far
from its nest,
its immaculate wing
held out to her awkwardly like a shy hand.

She refuses to nourish a lie,
cannot fabricate even four hours
of fairy tale until nightfall,
immediately locates a paper grocery bag
in which the terrified bird
rattles like a handful of dry leaves.
She must start the car despite her son's small,
firm grip on her arm,
close the bag's open end
over the exhaust pipe,
and it is not for her son's comfort
that she says:
It is better this way.)

Her husband, on the other hand,
will often wear underwear on his head

for comic effect.
But she sees his belly swelling,
knows where her men deposit their rage
so they might walk through a room
and not shatter everything
every day.

Can she bear
to bear witness again?

Love poem

Your brother has left his wife,
fallen for a younger woman.
We could be watching the re-run
of a made-for-TV-movie right now.
Only the hinge plot is missing:
redemption, revenge or madness,
temporary or otherwise, are all possibilities.

We watch and grope for the least intrusive advice possible—
take your time, breath, take your time—
hang up the phone with our mouths full of words
we then speak to each other.

A good crisis draws us together.
A good crisis is one that doesn't happen to us.
We know we are looking into one possible mirror.
We know our minds have already dressed in those clothes.
Scene One: door slams, much weeping, a new life
lived clear and free. Cut. Scene One: door slams, forgiveness.
Cut. Scene One: regret regret regret. Cut.
There's only ever a Scene One.

You can't judge from the photographs
because we are always smiling.
There was no one there to record
my weeping deep in the hay.
There was no one to record your hands
as they threw my great-grandfather's screen against the wall.
There is no photograph of the first night
we slept apart in anger, or the next.

Falling in love was like a sickness,
my yearning for you so strong and constant and
I was by nature so solitary there came a point I nearly
couldn't abide it, that sudden dependence on your voice,
on the way you held my face in your hands.

I know your body better than I know my own,
know your face better than I know my own,
the scars on your lips,
the minute folds of skin beneath your ears.
I spend my days believing
that these belong to me.

Red Volkswagen

It was right out in the parking lot next to the
dumpster—here I'll—

Listening from the phone in her lap I hear
my mother wheeling across the dining room,
hear the alarm whoop as she opens the outside door,
listen as she mutters *shit shit shit.*

Two days ago, or six weeks or months—or yesterday
it was taken, smashed up, hidden
or borrowed without permission.
Today my brother is the culprit.
She never says: *Why do you collude?*
She might still need me, for one thing or another.

All those years of silent bridge strategies
spiralling wildly out hand after hand,
of reading her partner's bluff in a seven of diamonds,
of positioning herself to gobble up all the trump.
She imagines herself in me—plotting.

Trace me backwards, skull collapsing briefly to re-enter the womb,
hands reverting to paddles, eyes milking over,
spine a comma, a pause—
and before that a code waiting deep within her body
without patience or impatience.
So the hand writing these words
can indeed be seen as the stuff of her own hand.

Once this hand would have cast nets,
dug traps, locked her in a room walled with mirrors
until she could see me.
But that was long ago.

How like a nightmare for her to wake up daily
in a stranger's body, a stranger's life.
How dreamlike it must be when she speaks,
seeing clearly how everyone nods in agreement
and no one believes a word she says.

I extend my compassion across thousands of miles,
and from a safe remove.

How to begin

How to begin again and again?
All that must happen for eyes to flutter open,
spine to heave erect, legs to swing over,
feet to recoil then resettle against a cold floor.

How many hundreds of thousands of dishes washed
after the mouth opens again and again
for the bread, the soup, after it swirls
the first taste of wine around the tongue?
The telephone answered again and again, how many times
I'm fine? How many times the pencil grasped,
how many headlines suddenly ten years old?

Again and again the sun leaps above the dark swathe of forest.
Each morning cedar and spruce, paper birch, striped maple
wait to be relieved of dew or frost or snow.

This waking before sunrise,
everything equal in silt and shadow.
The trees dark and waiting,
the wind caught deep in dawn's gullet.
This, the world perched on day's coming edge.
The moment the sun's lip closes
on that frozen crest of hill,
crystal with nettle and thistle.

My night-thick body and muddy eyes
can behold all this from behind
a never-washed window
and all is new again—
as long as the heart can crack and scar,
bear the world into the world
just one more day.

Dukkha (suffering)

Here is the plateau of ease.
The children are nearly raised,
nearly unharmed.

Finally, the marriage was too distracted to fall
apart. Now it simply takes too much effort
not to love each other.

Knowledge has accumulated. One is perceived
as containing expertise. A considerable salary
from a genuine job deposits itself twice monthly.

It slowly dawns that furniture can be afforded.
There is the possibility of an addition.
A room filled with light.

From this height the future can be seen to arrive,
rolling towards you across a wide, flat plain
and all approaching disturbances are visible.

How even the last cut of hay, so fragrant
in late afternoon sun,
even the mornings, the mist,
the rushing creek,
even the sky filled with hundreds of geese,
their cacophony grounded by you, vibrating in you,
flying so low, even their pale belly feathers,
even the wood in your mouth of wild apple, you
and the bear stunned in each others' paths,
even the ridge, the sudden Appalachians

before, behind, around—

how none of even this.

The wilderness in you wanting out.

Residuum

There are certain rooms currently closed.
For example, "I," with its mellifluous arcana.
Its rococo flabbergast.

"Us" a perpetual renovation.
Parry struggle define define relent accost sublimate.
Winds that once and sometimes blow through that space.

All the while gratitude spreading unbidden
beneath our feet.

Then what?

The articulation of leaves.
The watery percussion of arteries.
The shining heart.

Your voice speaking through mine—
through everything.

Grandmother, sewing

For Elisabeth Engler

Like some exquisite animal from a Chinese fairy tale—
silky black enamel and stainless steel polished silver,
and silver the threading arm,
dropping down then arching up to the spool, a goose
unfurling its neck over and over.
The hum when your foot
in its small sequinned slipper
commanded the treadle,
the needle dipping down, tasting the warp
and weave again, again.

My own fingers are dumb to this work.
Thick and knuckled,
they can't guide the slippery fabric,
or hold the tension steady.
Those are languages encoded in a wrist my fingers
will never bend enough to reach. No—
these dull blunt fingers caught to ropy hands
cannot reach you there
on the hard cushion of your sewing bench.
They cannot touch the amber beads, the thin neck,
the earthbrown shirt, the softening face.

Still, they nearly reach
the smell of your perfume,
your kindness,
the way your comb felt in my hands
when last I smoothed your hair.

Winter forecast

Wind will huddle by the pond,
trees will gather the air greedily around
until it creases,
snow will ice and crust.

But right now
the sun is slow and thick,
birds still sing,
I have had numerous visits from bees.

Sometimes possibility doesn't mean the future.
Sometimes it means the yellow of these leaves
strung on thread, looped from a braid of dogwood
hanging over the kitchen table.

Sometimes it means the noise leaves make
before the sweet fresh wind
lifts the curls at the back of your neck
and sniffs you there to see if you belong.

First birth

In the photograph there is blood
and mayhem, standard issue for an ordinary birth.
The walls, as you can imagine, fairly pulse
with abrupt discovery of the unknown,
of the unexpected expected.

Just beyond the camera frame, out the slick edge
of reflecting window lies the night,
sharp and tight as late December nights will be,
and utterly, utterly quiet for
moments at a time.
Frigid air clutches sounds—
abrupt conversations of dogs farm to farm,
boards on the barn shrinking,
two geese far from open water.

And higher still
water vapour condenses and billows,
races itself around the earth, rises,
falls, drops—always seeking the ocean
before rising again toward the stars,

and among the stars are silences unthinkable as time,
black holes that will pull you into the future
even as they stretch you apart
upon the cusps of their horizons—

and so back to that, the cusp
and the child being pulled back
into the room,
the ordinary room
with its imperfect paint and dirty windows,
its walls patient in their willingness
to absorb this moment intact.

First child leaves home

It has just been a matter of learning to breathe
differently. From the fingers in, say.

Of calibrating the ventricles to accept this shift
in oxygen without your breath in it.

It has just been a matter of eroding the body's
memory, its leaning, a morning's first kiss.

There has been some considerable explaining to the arms,
which are slow to grasp the parameters of absence.

When you fail to turn in your bed, the feet,
tentative in this larger silence, navigate stairs.

The hands do what is necessary to heat water,
steep flowers. The throat remembers

to swallow. Some day the body will
not be thick with this new language.

It will invert what should be inverted.
It will negate what should be negated.

Some day the body will not confuse its subject and object.
It will decline and agree without forethought.

This is not the first time the body has woken as a foreigner
because of you. Once the night was perfectly still,

perfectly cold. Once I saw you
take in your first breath

and was transformed.

What remains

Be careful that it is not
only dust between floorboards,
orphan screws clustering on window ledges
like hollow winter flies,
drawings drawn,
dishes washed.

Let it be the memory of a gesture
in a difficult moment,
the brush of lips when the red and yellow leaves
rattle the air like rain,
the belly laugh of nothing in particular.

Your gesture as it slips into our boys' bodies,
making their hands move to their chins
like this

Acknowledgments

Poems from *The Truth of Houses* have appeared in the following magazines and journals: *The Awakenings Review, Brick Magazine, Contemporary Verse 2, The Dalhousie Review, Event, The Malahat Review, The Mississippi Review, The Mitre, The New Quarterly, Prairie Fire, PRISM international, Room of One's Own,* and *Taproot I, II,* and *IV.*

The excerpts from *The Timeless Way of Building* by Christopher Alexander (1979) appear by permission of Oxford University Press, Inc.

This book began one way several years ago and ended up this way because of support, companionship and advice from the following writers: Carolyn Rowell, Marjorie Brumheller, Brenda Hartwell and Ellen Goldfinch; Betty Buchsbaum and Sara Reinstein; Michael Ondaatje; Ashok Ferrey and Vivimarie Vander Poorten; Michelle Ariss; Alayna Munce. Sometimes it was noticing, sometimes insisting, sometimes a gesture. Thank-you.

In addition, a special thanks to David Robson and the Geoffrey Bawa Trust for permission to use the images that illustrate these pages. The draughtsman for the image on page 11 is Anura Ratnavibushana. The draughtsman for the image on page 65 is Chana Daswatte.

Ann Scowcroft has been a professional writer and editor for many years, and was an academic for a few. She has a PhD in Applied Linguistics and presently works in the field of humanitarian assistance. Quebec is home base. *The Truth of Houses* is her first book.